POST
EARLY
Hoffnung

THE HOFFNUNG SYMPHONY ORCHESTRA

By the Author of

THE MAESTRO
THE HOFFNUNG MUSIC FESTIVAL
THE HOFFNUNG COMPANION TO MUSIC
HOFFNUNG'S MUSICAL CHAIRS
HOFFNUNG'S ACOUSTICS

BIRDS, BEES AND STORKS
HOFFNUNG'S LITTLE ONES
HOFFNUNG'S CONSTANT READERS

HO HO HOFFNUNG

The Hoffnung Symphony Orchestra

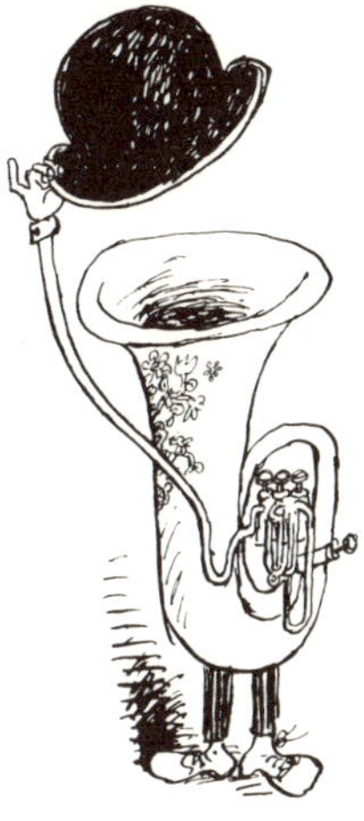

by

Gerard Hoffnung

London : Dennis Dobson

First Published March 1955
Second Impression June 1955
Third Impression (revised edition) November 1955
Fourth Impression February 1957
Fifth Impression October 1957
Sixth Impression June 1958
Seventh Impression June 1960
Eighth Impression November 1962
Ninth Impression December 1968
Tenth Impression December 1972
Eleventh Impression October 1975

I would like to express my thanks to Messrs. Bradbury, Agnew & Co., Ltd., proprietors of PUNCH, and to Hulton Press Ltd., for publishing in advance some of the drawings in this book. *G.H.*

Printed in Belgium by
Henri Proost & Co p.v.b.a.
Published in Great Britain by
Dobson Books Ltd
80 Kensington Church Street, London, W.8

ISBN 0 234 77354 5

THE STRINGS

The Violin (Leader)

The Violon Double

The Viola

The Viola Pizzicato

The Yo-Bow

The Cello

The Double Bass (a left handed player)

The Piccolo Double Bass

The Harp

The String Tuba

This instrument is sometimes referred to as the "Minstrel Tuba" or the "Blow-Plucker". It is interesting to note that the String Tuba is a member of both the string and brass families though it is usually seated with the former.

The Zither

The Piano (Boudoir Grand)

The Spanish Guitar

The Ondes Martenot

THE WOODWIND

The Flute and the Piccolo Flute

The Bass Flute

SUITE.

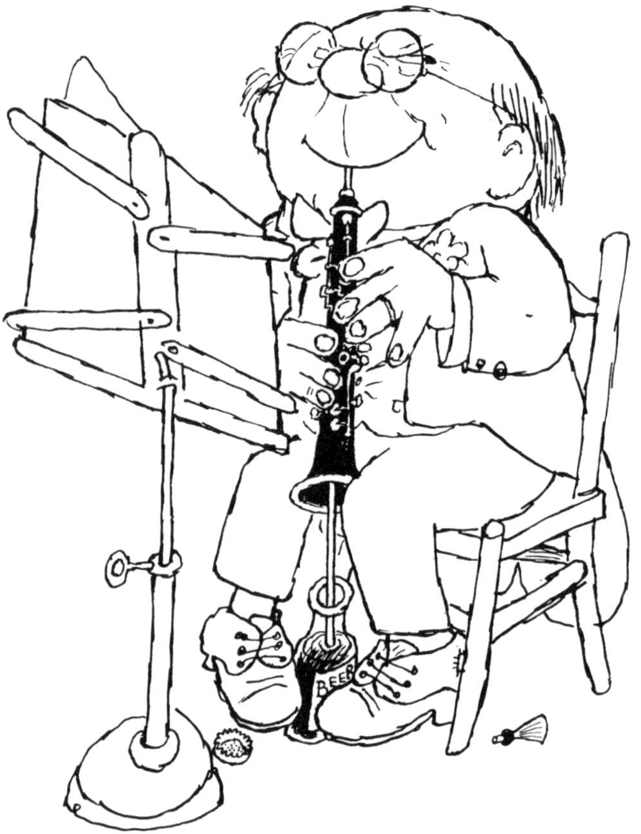

The Oboe

The Cor Anglais

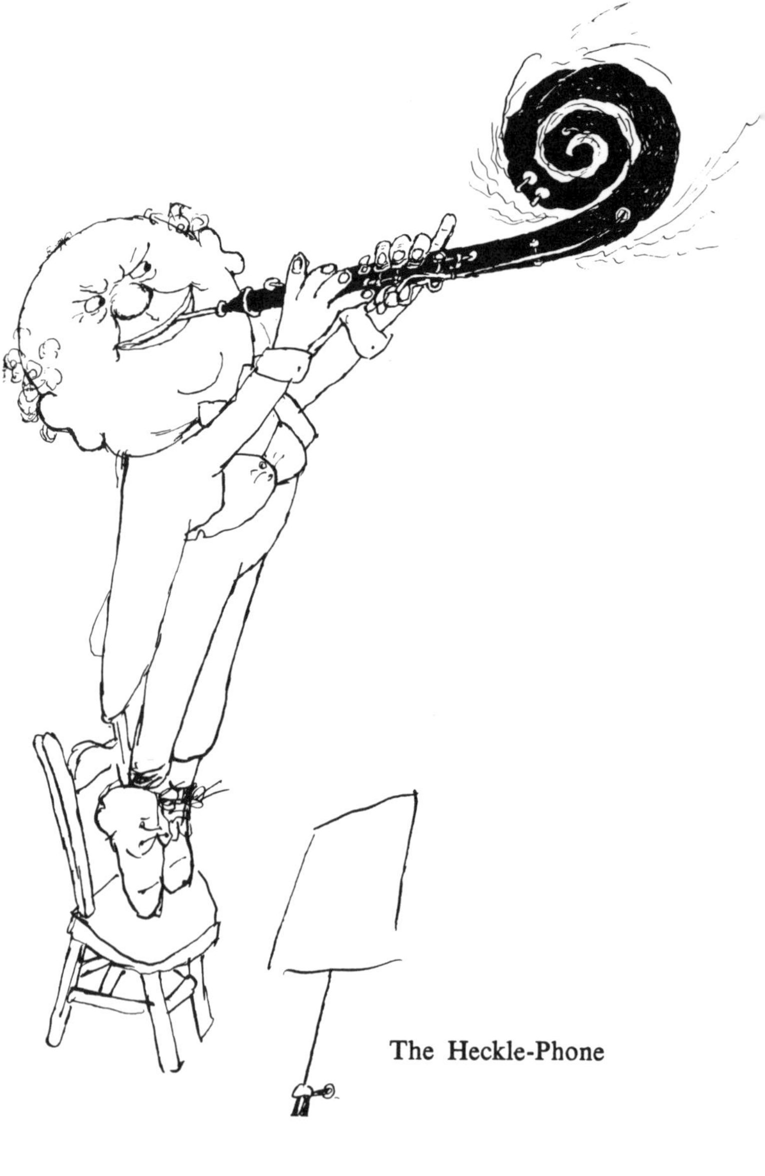

The Heckle-Phone

The Clarinet and the Bass Clarinet

The Saxophone

The Bassethorn

The Bassoon

The Contra-Bassoon

The Organ

THE BRASS

The Horn

The Trinkler

The Double Trumpet

The Serpent

For security reasons this instrument is no longer in use.

The Trombone

The Bass Trombone

The Wagner Tuba

The Bass Tuba

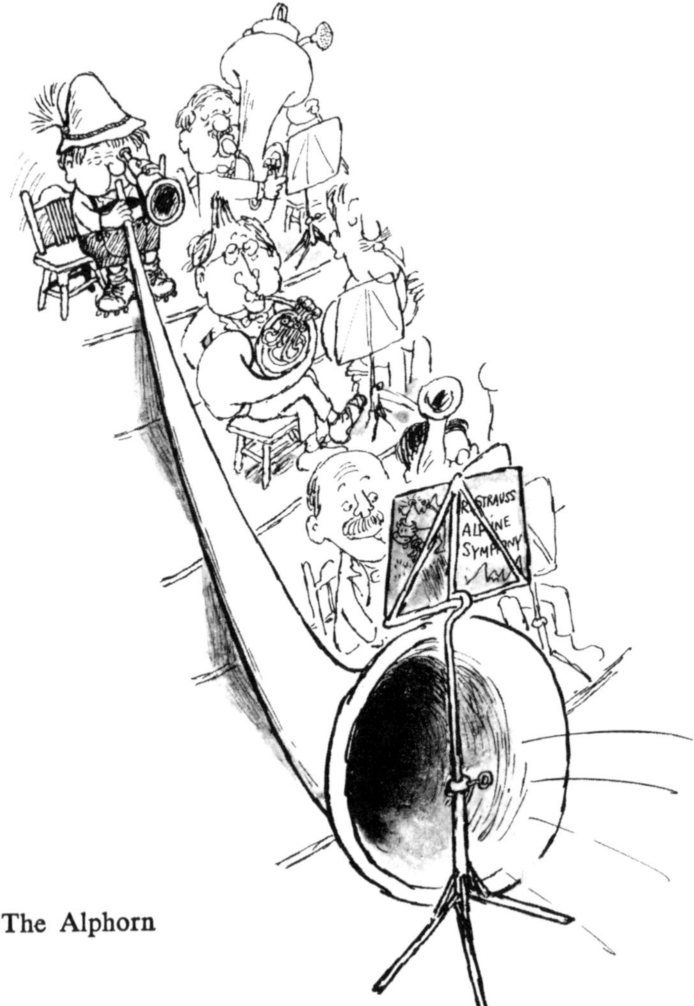

The Alphorn

THE PERCUSSION

The Timpani

The Cymbals

The Side Drum

The Bass Drum

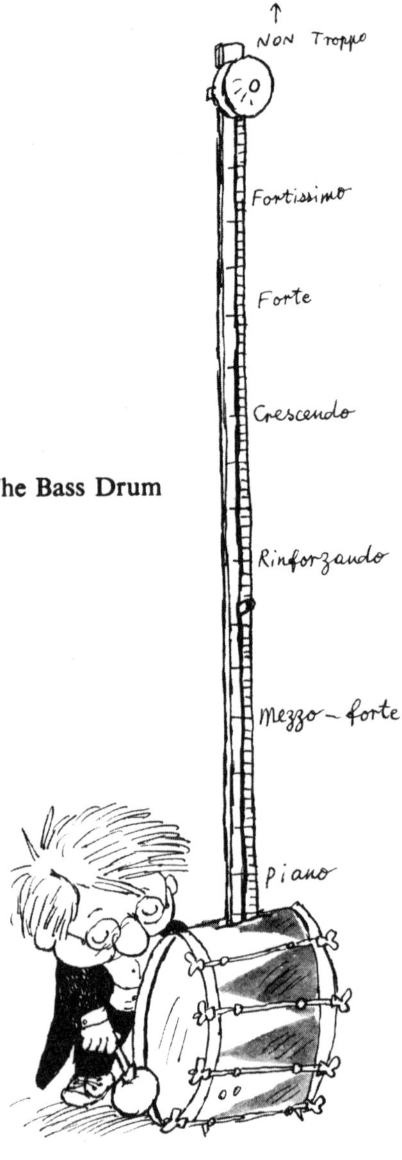

The Tum Drum

The Tubular Bells

The Triangle

The Xylophone

The Vibraphone

The Celeste

The Jingle Bells and the Chinese Block

The Wind Machine

Don Quixote
by
Richard Strauss

The Gong and the Tam Tam

The Castanets

END